CHAPTER ONE

The Beginning

A number of years ago, there was a TV show titled "*The Naked City.*" It always ended with this comment: "There are eight million stories in the Naked City; you have just seen one of them." I have always wanted to leave something behind in writing or some type of media to let my children or whomever know what it was like when I was growing up in the 1940s and 1950s. A number of years ago, there was a Focus on the Family insert in our church bulletin. One of the articles in this insert was titled "Preserving Your Family Heritage," by Dr. James Dobson. You can ask my wife or other close relatives, and they would say that I could have written this article. A portion of that article is quoted:

> The lyrics of an African folk song say that when an old person dies, it's as if a library has burned down. It is true. There's a richness of family heritage in each person's life that will be lost if it isn't passed on to the next generation. The stories of your past, of your childhood, of the courtship with your spouse, and so on can be treasures to your children. Unless you share those experiences with them, that part of their history will be gone forever. Take the time to make yesterday come alive for the kids in your family.

My grandmother left hundreds of pictures without names or dates. Some people would mark a photo with a name Sally, age three, or Tom, sixth grade. What year was it when Sally was three: 1932, 1946, 1989? Or what year was it when Tom was in the sixth grade? Take the time to date and name photographs, events, news clippings, etc., when it first happens. Don't trust your memory until tomorrow.

Before the age of digital photos, we all had hard copies of photos stored in shoe boxes, albums, drawers, etc. I have thousands of photos in albums and another thousand or so in slides. I have all the albums numbered and a summary index of the people or places in the photos on my computer. All my photos are stored in a clothes closet near the entrance/exit of the house. My instructions to all our children are in the event of a fire, each person is to grab photo albums on their way out of the house. My second son, Elliot, was visiting us one day with one of Nebraska's assistant football coaches. I explained my system to Jimmy; a few days later, Elliot saw Jimmy at Walmart. Jimmy told Elliot, "Your dad really made me think; I am here buying photo albums." I have since digitalized the important shots of the hard copies and slides. Of course, all digitals are backed up online. What we leave behind for the next generation is for that generation to decide what they will do with it. If they do nothing, then at least they will have passed it on. Was it important that someone left a note about George Washington chopping down a cherry tree?

In order to tell the story about Uncle Little Buddy, I have to tell the story of others as well, beginning with my life and my maternal grandparents. Any information about my paternal grandparents came from what my dad and/or his sister, Mittie, told me.

CHAPTER TWO

Growing up in Arkansas

Where I was born and grew up in Arkansas was almost like watching the "chase" in an old Western movie. If you pay close attention, you will notice some of the zigzags covered the same area that you saw a few zigzags ago. As I grew older, I was quite surprise to find out that those moves we made really didn't take us that far away, just a few miles to another cotton field. From 1941 to 1951, we moved approximately six times, and they all were within six to ten miles of each other. We were to make three more moves before I left Arkansas. The first one was to a farming community called "33" and the other two on the same plantation, less than a mile between all three houses. The last one was to the "white house." I will explain more about this move later.

My father, Roy Phillips, along with his brother, Joe, and two sisters, Mittie and Pearle, was born to Lela Thomas (1886–1927) and her husband, near Alexandria, Louisiana. Mittie was born in 1912; Roy on January 30, 1913; and Joe and Pearle a couple of years later. Dad did not talk about a father or a stepfather. Either their parents divorced or the father died. I have heard it both ways. In any event, the kids were young when the father was no longer part of their lives. Mittie remembered the name real well, but unfortunately, she could not spell it and the pronunciation was very difficult to understand. It sounded like "Donnell or Donald." I have a videotape of her trying to pronounce it so it could be understood. The Phillips name as it pertains to this family only goes back to about 1917 or 1918. Their mother married a man named Charley Phillips, who adopted her children. Or they were just given his name; thus, we became "Phillips." Charley died in 1922.

The new Phillips's children left this world in reverse order in which they came. Pearle, the youngest, whom I never knew died first in the 1930s, then Joe in 1941, Roy in 1984, and then Mittie in 1996. To my knowledge, the sisters did not have any children. Joe had one daughter, named Ruby Jean. We knew Ruby very well. She even lived with us for a brief period. Ruby and my oldest sister Roberta did their part in increasing the Phillips's clan. They both had ten or twelve children each.

During his early years, Dad lived a rough life, according to the way he described his many adventures. He could do many different types of jobs, from plowing mules to driving eighteen wheelers. He would try just about anything, except trying to educate himself. Somewhere along the way, he did learn how to write his name. Watching *The Fugitive* on TV reminded me of my dad: He toiled at many jobs.

Mittie remembered that Dad's name was not Roy, but James Leroy Phillips, but he did not like the "James Lee," so somewhere along the way he became known as Roy. However, he named their oldest son James Lee. He talked a lot about his mother and the adventures they had growing up with her and her father, his grandfather. He couldn't sing, but he loved to try and sing that old hymn "If I Could Hear My Mother Pray Again." I recall Dad telling us stories about his mom raising them, even how she shot a man one night who was stealing her chickens. She heard a noise in the chicken house. Thinking it was an animal, she grabbed her shotgun; and as she walked out of the house, the man took off running. She shot at the sound of his feet hitting the ground, wounding him, but not killing him. The next day she went to the boss man's house and told him what had happened. The man was found later and was severely admonished for trying to steal from "the widow woman." There were other stories about his grandfather.

One particular story was how they had been scared by a possible attack from a panther. That same afternoon, his grandfather gathered supplies; mounted his horse, leading a packhorse; and took off in search of the panther. The next day his grandfather appeared with a long black dead panther draped over the packhorse. There were never any stories about a father or stepfather.

Dad told a lot of stories about his rambling from place to place, mostly traveling by hopping trains, hitchhiking, and working all kinds of jobs. This left very little time for any kind of formal schooling and/or training. Roy, Mittie, and Joe eventually settled in northeastern Arkansas, in and around St. Francis County. It is not known if their mother, Lela, and sister, Pearle, died while they lived in Louisiana. Joe married a lady, named Essie Richmond. As mentioned earlier, they had one daughter, Ruby Jean, born on December 6, 1939, and a son who died before he was one year old. Roy married Mozelle Williams. They had four children, James, Roberta, and a set of twins. Mozelle and the twins died in early 1937. The flood of 1937 in eastern Arkansas could have been a contributing factor to their death. April of that year, Roy married Alice McDonald, my mother. She was born on February 20, 1920. He was twenty-four, and she was seventeen. Daddy used to tell the story of how he and my mother eloped. He bought the marriage license on a Saturday and showed them to her at church that Sunday. The following Sunday she never returned home from church. Grandpa Willie was told whom they saw her leave church with. He got his shotgun and went looking, but luckily he never found them. After not finding them, it was said that he just blasted a few rounds in the nearby lake.

Roy and Alice had eight children: Arthur, Cleopatra, Ruby (same name as Joe's daughter), Charles, Lee, Maeola, Melverdia, and the baby boy who was stillborn at the time of Alice's death in 1952. Mother started off with a four- and a two-year-old. Just think; she was only seventeen. Eleven months after the marriage, March 7, 1938, I was born in a farming area on Arkansas State Highway 50, between Widener and Hughes, Arkansas. The actual post office address was Round Pond, Arkansas. I was her oldest. Fifteen months later, my sister Cleopatra was born, and they kept coming.

In 1942, we lived close to a railroad track, not far from an area called Whitmore. Those were the days of long trains with cabooses. We would wave to the engineers when they came by and then waited to wave to the men in the caboose. All those songs about railroads help me keep memories alive. Jimmie Rodgers's songs about railroads are my favorite. In the 1960s, Gogi Grant recorded a song that helps rekindle the memories, "The Wayward Wind." One day while we were living there, Dad came home from working in the field, and the dog ran to meet him. What I thought was a gesture of gladness to see him, but the dog bit Dad on the thigh, taking a small plug out. Dad went in the house, came out with his shotgun, and shot the dog dead right before us. It must have had some kind of effect on me because I never forget how the dog's collar just flew off at the impact from the shot.

In 1943 we moved to a community called McNeil's Farm, still on Highway 50. A lot of things happened during that year. My oldest brother, James, was now ten; and my oldest sister, Roberta, was eight. I think that was the first time either one of them ever attended school. It was the last time my brother James attended any kind of school. Mom and Dad had many disagreements concerning them going to school. She insisted that they go to school, and he thought they should work in the fields. My brother Charles was born on April 1 of that year. A young man whom we knew as Mr. S. A. was part of the McNeil's household; I don't know what the relationship was. Periodically, he would drive to our house, perhaps to interact with my dad. The friendliness that he always showed to us children still lingers in my memories today. He landed a small airplane in a hay field close to our house. This was the first time I had ever seen a plane on the ground.

The plantation house in 1943, still standing in 2017

Portrait of Mr. S. A.

I don't recall when; it could have been shortly after we left this farm or it could have been a year or two later that we were told that Mr. S. A had been killed in the war somewhere overseas. It was a sad occasion for all of us. Whenever I visit that part of Arkansas, I make it a priority to visit all the old landmarks I knew as a child. It was in 2006 when I made such a visit to the old plantation house. As in previous visits, the house was vacant, except for one year; it was being used for some type of retail, pottery, garden supplies, etc. However, when I made the visit in 2006, there was a lady whose name is Amie Devereux who was at the house. She or her husband was related to Mr. McNeil and Mr. S. A. We had quite a chat about the history of the farm. She and her husband were in the process of refurbishing the house. As I was telling her some memories of my childhood there, and the story of Mr. S. A., she agreed with me as to what kind of a gentleman he was and invited me in to view a large portrait of Mr. S. A. The portrait was exactly the way I had remembered him.

The Staple Singers recorded a song titled "Back Road into Town," which identified with poor sharecroppers. It was a common practice for sharecroppers, as we were, to harvest a crop of cotton and move on to another farm the following year, still owing the previous "boss man" money, so their books indicated. For us there was a different farm each year. This could have been the case that caused Dad to flee to Chicago in late 1943. He returned late that year or in early 1944. It was strange how he slipped in the house one night and stayed a couple of days and one night slipped out again back to Chicago. During those couple of days, he never went outside of the house during the daytime. I learned later that his intent was to move all of us to Chicago. Apparently things did not work out in Chicago, probably because he could not read and write. He would have had problems supporting a wife and six children. Shortly after he departed a second time, Mom and the children went to live with Big Mama (my maternal grandmother) a few miles away. It seemed that only a couple of months later, Dad was back in Arkansas. We continued to stay with Big Mama for another few weeks, and then we all, including Big Mama's family, moved to a community called Rollinson, on a farm owned by Doctor Chaffin.

We lived close to Big Mama and Papa throughout my preteen and teen years. By the time they moved a distance away, I could drive, and transportation had taken on a new dominion. This is where we were living when the news came about Uncle Little Buddy.

We, the children of Alice, felt that we had a heads-up on the other nieces and nephews because our mother was Uncle Buddy's twin sister. She used to tell plenty of stories about their childhood. Well, this is the primary reason I am writing these memoirs or this book. I will get to Uncle Little Buddy later. Some people have questioned my ability to remember things. They say that I was too young to remember some events that I used to recall. I can remember being in bed as a baby and my older brother and sister were dancing on the floor, celebrating their new shoes. I write this to say that you can keep any memory alive by simply remembering and talking about it often.

In 1946 we moved from Rollinson to an area that was called "33." It is located between Hughes and Widener, closer to Widener, on Arkansas State Highway 38. All farming communities had a name or number. Kids, school teachers, doctors, etc., knew what you meant when you gave the name or number. Again, the McDonalds (my grandparents) made the same move. A Chinese man whose name was Chie Fong owned the farm. I recall he and Dad were of the same age, thirty-three. We thought it was funny to have a "boss man" and a dad aged thirty-three and live in "33."

There was a period each year called "the settlement date," which meant about 75 percent of the cotton had been gathered, and the boss would open the books and count how much of your cotton he had sold, take his portion, and subtract how much money you owed him. Most of the time, you were still in the red, not so with Chie. That first year and each subsequent year, almost all the farmers made money on the first settlement, and there was still more money to be made from the cotton that was still in the fields. This was home for most of the children from Dad's first two marriages until they were grown and began to make their trek on life. It was during this period that Dad seemed to have been very happy. One year he even played baseball, and we would often travel to Memphis to watch the Memphis Red Sox play.

It was sometime during this period that Mom's oldest brother, Earnest, and dad had been drinking in Hughes where they got into a heated disagreement that continued after they had reached our house. My oldest sister was stirring the fire in the heater when Dad approached her and said, "Let me have the poker. You are not doing it right." At that same time, Uncle Earnest sensed what Dad's intention was when he went to take the iron poker from my sister, so he grabbed for the poker also. I don't know who won the battle of the iron poker, but somehow Dad came up with a claw hammer and caused quite a bit of bodily damage on Uncle Earnest. Shortly after this incident, Dad expected retaliation, because a pistol showed up at the house.

Highway 38 was gravel at that time. We lived about three hundred yards off the highway on a dirt road. Between our house and the highway was a small patch of brushes and trees on both sides of this dirt road. Any period of heavy rain, the truck had to be parked near the gravel road. Mom said that Dad used to walk home at night with the pistol in his hand looking from side to side. This incident obviously caused some strife between my grandparents and Dad, so they moved on to another farm near Heth, Arkansas.

Arkansas Highway 38

My mom died on May 1, 1952, at the young age of thirty-two after giving birth to her eighth child, which was stillborn. I often think about the situation. She had given birth to the other seven children at home with assistance of a midwife. She went to the hospital to have number 8. I don't think any problem was anticipated. I just think that midwives were becoming a thing of the past. The baby was stillborn, and she died shortly thereafter, about 11:45 p.m. I don't know why I wasn't in school that day. I do know I was driving a tractor that morning, plowing cotton or preparing the ground for planting some type of crop. I had driven my tractor to the house that afternoon, perhaps to get a drink of water or something. As I was about to mount my tractor, she had walked down the steps from the porch and was walking toward Dad's pickup. She looked up at me smiling and said, "I will see you, boy." I acknowledged her. As I drove off on the tractor, I saw them drive away in the truck. That was the last time I saw her alive. Dad took her to Hughes and went to Parkin to pick up her mother. It was normal for Big Mama to be with her when she was giving birth. That night, shortly after midnight, Dad came to our room first. Charles, Lee, and I slept in the same bed. I repeat, same bed. The bright overhead light came on; "Mom is dead" were the chilly words from Dad as he stood over us. We didn't have time to respond before I heard Roberta's feet, my oldest sister, in the joining room hit the floor, as she began to scream.

I don't know what happened the rest of the night. I think I immediately went into what we now call denial. For the next few days leading up to the funeral, I just expected to see her walking through the door. I had heard about Jesus raising people from the dead. I thought that perhaps he would raise her. I was fourteen at the time. I don't know if I prayed or not. Besides, praying was for the older people. Children only prayed the Lord's Prayer, so I thought.

Home when Mom died in 1952

In fourteen short years, my mom was a great influence in my life, even to this day. When my two oldest sons call their mother for whatever reason, I think it must be nice. But when I see mothers like my friend Lonnie Hyter's mother who is in her nineties, I also think it's nice, because I have gone through what he has to face. When I was a teenager, this older man, who I supposed was in his seventies, passed away after being ill for a few months. The next morning, a friend by the name of Howard Hardrick and my dad were discussing the death of Mr. Humphrey when Howard made the comment: "I wish I could trade places with him." Dad understood what Howard was talking about right away, but they had to explain it to me in detail. Howard went on to explain that Mr. Humphrey had already done what he has to do, that is, to die.

When school started that summer in 1952, I did not return. My dad being uneducated really did not believe in it. He now had me full time to work on the farm five and six days per week. On Saturdays

I would work at Mr. Fong's grocery store, stocking shelves, cleaning, bagging, and taking out groceries. During the last two years, I worked as the butcher. We would work from 8:00 a.m. to after midnight. Then, Gin, the oldest son who was the store's boss, would lock the doors; and we would pitch pennies until almost daybreak. After a few months, we went from pennies to nickels and on to playing penny poker, and naturally that graduated to higher stakes. By the time I was fifteen, I could do most things that grown men could do, including driving all the farm equipment, trucks, and cars. I was even smoking cigarettes. Thank, God, I didn't like the taste of booze and beer. I liked the taste of that cheap wine, but I was told that stuff would drive you crazy; some said that you are already crazy if you drank it. I believed them and stayed away from wine also. By now I was avoiding school teachers because I knew a lecturer would be coming. But a teacher whose name was Johnnie Tyson finally cornered me somewhere in downtown Forrest City, a huge lady in size but of the no-nonsense type. The school staff and students respected her. To this day I give God the credit and glory for bringing her to me because she convinced me to return to school. I had dropped out when I was in the seventh grade and skipped all of the eighth. The classmates that I started junior high with were now freshmen. So I decided that I would just enroll myself in the eighth grade, and they allowed it. I went on to high school, played football and baseball, and received a football scholarship from Philander Smith College. During the summer of 1958, I visited my aunts in Davenport, Iowa. I returned home with the intention of going to college, but with no encouragement, I pitched the application in a drawer and went back to Davenport. In January 1959, I sent my high school sweetheart a bus ticket; and we were married on January 7, 1959. A few weeks later, I joined the Air Force, and my story continues.

During the early part of the twentieth century, almost all plantations consisted of a large white house where the "boss man" lived and a company store. Do you remember Tennessee Ernie's song with a line "I owe my soul to the company store"? In our situation, the boss was the foreman whose name was Lawrence Wilson. Also in this large house was a small grocery store. Everything burned to the ground in the late 1940s or early 1950s. The Wilsons lost everything. Mr. Fong, the owner of the farm, built a smaller white house in the same location. During the early 1950s, many of the large plantations in this part of eastern Arkansas also had a Negro in charge of several other Negro sharecroppers and day workers. Although Daddy was just another sharecropper, trying to feed a family like everyone else, he was soon thrust into that position while Mr. Wilson was the foreman. When the Wilsons left the farm in 1954, Daddy became the foreman, and we moved into the "white house." Mr. Fong really gave Dad the opportunity to show his skills in carpentry, mechanics, and overall farm management and, eventually, made him the foreman. As a matter of fact, Mr. Fong's honesty helped a lot of Negroes to prosper while working on his farm.

The white house in 1954

After Mom's death, Dad did a wonderful job of taking care and protecting us. The ability to look ahead and plan for the future just wasn't there. In addition, there were "the wine, women, and songs." But Solomon knew best: It was all vanity. I say that because Dad made good money back then, but it went through his hands just like dry sifting sand. He was uneducated and made many, many bad choices.

When I was about fifteen, the boss man's son, Gin, whom I worked for gave me a Kodak 620 camera that was slightly damaged. By placing tape over a crack, I was able to take snapshots. Later on I bought a new Kodak 127. Then somebody gave me a Kodak 120 and then a Kodak 116. At about age seventeen, I had five or six cameras. I even had one with a flash. I was always shooting pictures. By the time I left home and moved to Davenport, Iowa, there was quite a collection. I left all my snapshots and a few other personal things in a wooden box about a third the size of a military footlocker. A few months later, I returned to collect my things. My brothers and sisters who were still at home told me that dad had thrown the box away and everything in it. Dad said he didn't know what had happened to it. So that was my first loss of a piece of history in pictures and perhaps a few other things.

By the early 1970s, farming had taken a whole new twist in this area of Arkansas. Rice and other farm items had begun to replace cotton. This time, Dad would leave the farm for good. He and his third wife, Bernice, and their six children, Ella, Albert, Kenneth, Cherry, Carolyn, and Robert, along with the youngest from the second marriage, packed up and moved to Memphis. He might have become a city man, but he never gave up his pickup trucks. In 1947 he bought a 1941 Ford pickup that he was so proud of, and pickups were his trademark. He never owned a car. Roy left behind a legacy of hard work that was passed on to his children and grandchildren. At his funeral in April 1984, fourteen of his eighteen children were present. The twins from his first marriage, Ruby, and the son who was stillborn preceded him in death.

CHAPTER THREE

The McDonald Family

As mentioned earlier, the motivation behind what has been written and the remaining pages is because of the life of Allen Marion McDonald (Uncle Little Buddy) and a collection of pictures and papers found in his house after his death that was previously owned by his mother, my grandmother, which will be explained later. The story could not be complete without knowing about Uncle Buddy's parents, sibling, relatives, and other acquaintances, beginning with his parents.

His father, Isaac Willie McDonald, was born in Mississippi in 1896. His paternal grandfather was white, which means his paternal grandmother was a slave. He married Luella Curtis. To this union, they had eight children: Essie, Earnest (Cut), a set of twins Allen (Little Buddy) and Alice, James, Josephine (Josie), Ethel, Everlyn (Doll), and Thomas (T. C.).

The McDonalds, including Grandma Luella, whose maiden name was Curtis, were born in Mississippi, in a region called the "Delta." They moved to eastern Arkansas in 1933 to a community called "Blackfish Lake," between Forrest City and Hughes on Arkansas State Highway 50. In 1940 or 1941, they lived in a community called Stump City, close to Hughes and even closer to Greasy Corner, still on Arkansas State Highway 50. After Dad returned from Chicago, they also moved to Rollinson.

Essie, the oldest of the siblings, married John Henry Crawford. They had fourteen children: John Jr., Dorothy, Erna, Vernon, Herman, Lester, Harold, Arnold, Kenneth, Cordell, Menard, Carolyn, Cheryl, and Joan Marie.

One year when Aunt Essie visited us when we lived in McNeil's Farm, John Jr. and his sisters Dorothy and Erna were dressed so nice and clean. I was only five at the time, but I could tell they were different from us. They even talked different. I envied them, even that white "Navy-type cap" John Jr. was wearing. Dorothy and Erna wore some of the shortest dresses I had ever seen. Uncle John Henry, whom I never recall seeing until 1958, left Arkansas shortly after they were married. I think he got into some kind of trouble and had to flee Arkansas and, like many Negroes who fled the south, ended up in Chicago. He was big and strong. When Dad was living with them in 1943, Dad said that Uncle John came home one day mad because Aunt Essie had thrown away a letter he had written to Joe Lewis asking for a match. I don't know if he ever pursued it further. I think it was his fists that caused him to flee Arkansas.

Of all the Crawfords, Lester was the only one that committed an act that still stands out to me this day. It was 1948 or 1949 when Aunt Essie had come down to visit Big Mama with all her children. Lester was a toddler at the time. Outside, like most old farm housing, there were dogs in and/or around the houses. Big Mama had a dog chained up. It could have been chained to protect the children. Several warning went out to all the children to watch Lester and not let him go near the dog, because the dog might bite him. Again and again, the warning went out. Some time had passed, and it had gotten rather quiet. When all of a sudden, there came this sound from outside of a dog barking and screaming. Several of us ran out the door, and there was Lester with a "bear hug" on the dog and constantly burying his teeth into the dog's flesh.

I knew Uncle Earnest as a young man, but not very much as we both grew older. I think the last time I saw him was about 1965. I hitched a ride on an Air Force plane that was taking cadets athletics team from Denver to Des Moines. From Des Moines, I took a bus to Davenport. It was real early in the morning when I arrived in Davenport, and I didn't want to go to anyone's house that early. While I was standing on the street in front of the Greyhound Bus Station, he drove by and recognized me. He backed up and gave me a ride to Aunt Josie and J. C.'s house. To my knowledge, he had been married only once, and that was back in the early 1940s. I don't recall how the marriage was resolved.

Uncle James, the third oldest son, spent most of his adult life in the Chicago area. He would occasionally come back to Arkansas on long visits. Dad said that he would be hiding from the law. Dad really never had too much of anything good to say about Preacher Mac's sons (Papa McDonald) except Uncle Little Buddy. James was a very sharp dresser. He really looked good in his army uniform and civilian suits. Back in the 1940s, lots of young black men would have their hair "conked" (some type of chemical that would cause the hair to be kind of straight). They would use a stiff kind of hairdressing that would allow the hair to be combed and/or brushed back whereby it would show shiny black and wavy. As a kid, I thought that was cool. Needless to say, I looked forward to the day when I could do my hair that way, but it never came.

Uncle James got married for the first time while home on a furlough. I have forgotten the lady's name. I only saw her once or twice. She was a slim nice-looking lady. I don't know where she came from or where she went. To my knowledge, there were no children with this marriage.

After he left the Army, I don't know what kind of work he was in. My dad told me once that he was involved in robberies and hold-ups in the Chicago area. I didn't put much in that story. However, I do know that when his second wife died, he attended the funeral as a friend under an assumed name. I think that was due to some kind of welfare fraud. Even before his wife died, they were using different names. The last time I saw him was in late 1958 or early 1959. He came to the Blackhawk Hotel in Davenport and applied for a job. He asked me, and I gave him the OK to use my name as a reference for the job. It wasn't long after that I joined the Air Force. About two years later, I was notified that he had passed away. I was also told that the youngest brother, T. C., had made verbal threats about blowing up the hospital where Uncle James had died. I heard this from Big Mama. To my amazement, I got the feeling that she would have gone along with such nonsense.

Aunt Josephine, whom we called Josie, was the third oldest girl. I thought she was the most aggressive of all the McDonalds's women—aggressive in terms of not being satisfied with the status quo. She wanted and had a nice home, nice furniture, and nice car. She was not an educated woman, but believed in it wholeheartedly. I think all four of their children, Jim, Helen, Willie, and Doris, have at least one degree. Both boys were good athletes. Jim, whom we called Boogie, went to North Dakota University on a basketball scholarship. One of his teammates was Phil Jackson. In his senior year, he played football and was drafted and played a few years in the National Football League (NFL) with the New Orleans Saints and the Chicago Bears. I pay tribute to Jim for encouraging me to write this book. He passed away in November 2002 after a bout with lung and heart problems. There is an outstanding article written by Chuck Johnson about the University of North Dakota, two-sport athletes, Jim is featured in this article (www.undsports.com, search hall of fame, Jim Hester, 2/11/2008).

Aunt Josie's husband, J. C. Hester, treated me as if I was one of his sons. He was always impressed by the way Dad had raised us, and he often mentioned how tough our old man was. I was impressed with him as well. Almost like my dad, he also was uneducated. But in the middle forties when he arrived in the Quad Cities, he was able to land good jobs, which eventually led him to work for a long time for John Deere.

When I joined the Air Force, I received an assignment to Korea right after I completed technical school. Aunt Josie and J. C. took care of Dorothy while I was away. Actually it was a good trade-off because Dorothy never was a lazy person and she was great in helping in the upkeep of the house.

I sent J. C. a pipe from Korea, supposedly made of ivory. Dorothy wrote and told me how proud J. C. was of this pipe. He would sit on his front porch, cross or kick his legs up, and enjoy smoking his pipe. She didn't tell me until I had returned from Korea that one day he dropped his pipe and it broke. Dorothy said that it hurt him so bad. He asked her not to tell me because I would never send him anything again.

Ethel, daughter number 4, married Eddie Rose. They were divorced in less than ten years. Ethel was left to raise the two children: Vertice (Sonny) and Virginia (Ginny). Sonny was born with some type of mental disorder and had to spend most of his adolescent years and all of his adult life in group homes. He died in 2004. He was approximately forty-seven years old. Ginny died in 2004 at the age of about fifty-two. At the beginning of this writing, Ethel was the only sibling still living. A stroke caused her to be placed in a nursing home. For a number of years, she was unable to talk, but she maintained her cohesiveness. She began to talk a little a couple of years prior to her death. She still would not tell her age or answer many of the questions I asked her about the family. She passed away in September 2000 at the age of seventy, meaning she was born in 1930. It was something about the whole family when it came to passing information down to the children, even after the children became adults. Or maybe we were just too apathetic. Sonny or Ginny did not have any children which means Ethel's generation ended with the death of Ginny in 2004.

Aunt Evelyn (Doll), the youngest girl and I believe the only one of that generation to attend college, attended Philander Smith College, in Little Rock, Arkansas, for at least a year. For whatever reason, she left Arkansas for Davenport where she met and married Herman Goodwin. They had seven children: Herman, Sharon, Karen, Russell, Dietra (died shortly after birth), Timothy, and Mark. When I first visited Davenport in the summer of 1958, I stayed with them. They appeared to me to be a close-knitted family. Like the Hesters, they also owned a small neighborhood grocery store at one time. Herman, Doll's husband, was a few years older than her.

Actually, he was just a year younger than my mom. What a guy! He was a lot like Uncle Little Buddy as far as work ethics goes. He had so many high hopes that he often spoke about. Owning a store and owning a Cadillac were two of them, which he did accomplish. He worked at the Rock Island Arsenal, Illinois, and was in the National Guard. Herman had Alzheimer's the last few years of his life. He died in 2002.

Thomas Conway McDonald (he was mostly known as T. C. or T) was the youngest of that generation. He was two months older than me. He was his mother's baby, and he was a spoiled brat. He got just about everything that his mother could afford. I recall when we would go to the company's store with one or both of our parents, it seemed that he always got a pop, candy, and/or ice cream. Mom and Dad just could not afford such things with six children. In a footrace, he was much faster than I was. Sometimes he would run from Big Mama to avoid a spanking. Once he had done something and Big Mama reached to grab him and he took off. She made such an attempt to catch him I thought I would help. After which, she had given up and told him, "I will get you later." Later wasn't very long because I pretended I had something in my hand to give him. When he reached out his hand to take it, I grabbed him by his hand, screaming, "Here he is, Big Mama! Here he is!" I held on until she got there. It was nothing more than jealousy that caused me to deceive him. Another incident happened that I didn't have much of a choice but to tell on T. C. Papa owned four mules. He had stored up a huge stack of hay. It must have been about a 20-foot pole surrounded by a 20-foot circle of hay. As I watched from our house, I saw this puff of smoke coming from the base of the stack. Seconds later, I saw T make a quick dash from behind the hay toward the house. The girls and Big Mama tried to put the fire out, but couldn't pump water fast enough. As I look back, he probably could have been a good athlete. At age fourteen, he was almost six feet tall. He eventually grew to 6'3". All for naught, he quit school when he was about in seventh grade. As his mother put it, "T didn't like his teacher and wanted to quit, so I let him." This is the same lady that I wrote about earlier as believing in education, but not for her baby. By the time we reached our late teens, he was intellectually separated from most of the nieces, nephews, and peers due to his like of education. Unfortunately, in some cases he was ridiculed when he tried to converse with us about things of school. Big Mama allowed T to continue to have his way. This even began to show in his appearance. By the time they moved to Davenport, he had become more of a liability. In his lifetime he held very few jobs, mainly because of his lack of good hygiene. He owned a couple old vehicles that Big Mama bought for him, and then she had to pay him to take her places—places like the grocery store to buy food that he would eat also. Some people said that Big Mama lived as long as she did to ensure T was taken care of, because no one else would. By the time Big Mama died, T already had a brain tumor which he would not allow doctors to operate on. The tumor caused his death in 1991 at the age of fifty-three. I see that as a wasted life. It could have been worse. I never knew T to be into drugs or in any kind of trouble with the law. He always showed respect to people he met.

CHAPTER FOUR

The Discovery of Documents

Allen Marion McDonald, nicknamed Little Buddy, was a twin to Alice, my mother. He was the second oldest son, and Alice was the second oldest daughter. They were born on February 20, 1920. It is common to call a person by a nickname. I have heard of young black children going to school for the first time and not knowing their real name. I don't know why the name "Buddy." Our great uncle, Robert Bridges, was also called Buddy. In order to distinguish between the two, I suppose the younger one was called "Little Buddy." Alice passed away on May 1, 1952, and Allen in 1991.

I was too young to personally know Uncle Little Buddy prior to him being drafted, but many conversations and stories about him made me admire him. According to my mom, he was an early riser, even as a teenager. He did what had to be done without being told or watched. In other words, he was what we call in the Air Force "a self-starter." Mom said that Uncle Buddy was a hard worker. As a young boy, he was small in stature for his age. But Mom said that he was tough as nails. By the time he was twelve, he could pick two hundred pounds of cotton. Back then it was normal to say that a boy was ready for manhood if he could accomplish that feat. Most of the stories surfaced about him after he was drafted in the Army in 1942.

Prior to his death in 1991, Uncle Little Buddy apparently had appointed our cousin Ginny to oversee his estate. There wasn't really much to it, but Ginny milked it for all it was worth. She never allowed any of the other nieces and nephews to go into Uncle Buddy's house for several months after his death. Since I have always loved history, I really wanted those pictures; and if I had known about certain letters and papers that Big Mama possessed, I would have had to fight Ginny. Other relatives knew about the pictures but showed little interest in them. Apparently Ginny thought we wanted to search for other things. As it turned out, we could have probably found more history of the McDonald family. Ginny was preparing to sell the house in 1994, and the new owner was going to tear it down to make room for something else. It was now OK to go in the house. I believe my niece Cathy, who is very adventurous, was one, if not the first, beside Ginny to go in the house since Uncle Little Buddy's death.

My son Arthur Jr. who lived in Minneapolis was very much aware of how I wanted my grandmother's pictures. He also showed an interest in them and the history of our family. For whatever reason, he stopped over in Davenport en route to Chicago. He visited the house and called me after he had taken a look inside the house. From his description, the house was in terrible disarray. I found this to be true when I arrived and visited the house. It reminded me of the book of Nehemiah, whereby Nehemiah had sought permission from King Artaxerxes to travel to Jerusalem to repair the wall. When he had arrived, he found the wall and the city in ruin. The inside of Uncle Buddy's house wasn't too good before his death. But now you really felt as if you should wear a gas mask because of the filth and dust.

I was really motivated during this summer of 1994 and again about 2012, when I read a book by Eugene Richards, titled *Below the Line: Living Poor in America*. He wrote about the living condition in several cities/communities throughout the United States. One community was Hughes, Arkansas. This is the area where Uncle Little Buddy grew up. The movie *It's a Wonderful Life* really should cause everyone to take notes of their life of how it would have been if it wasn't for the "what ifs."

Arthur Jr., my sister Maeola, and my niece Cathy had already found some of the old pictures that Friday, the day before I arrived.

Arthur had described some of the pictures to me by phone, but the ones I really wanted were not among them. They even searched the house a second time to no avail. This was when I decided to drive to Davenport and see for myself, and I am glad I did.

My grandmother had this vast collection of pictures. Very few were marked with names or dates. Throughout my youth and even as an adult, I always looked at those pictures each time I would visit her and hoped that someday I would own them. She was placed in a nursing home in the 1980s. I asked Uncle Little Buddy about the pictures, and he said that they were in the possession of her youngest son, T. C. Big Mama died on March 3, 1989. T. C. died a year or two later. Shortly after T's death, I again asked Uncle Buddy about the pictures. He told me that they were in his basement with T's things, and when he got around to sorting things out he would let me know, but that never happened. There were two pictures I had particular interest in: one when I was about eighteen months old and one of my Dad when he was about thirty-four or thirty-five.

Arthur Jr. was at the house the next morning (Saturday). We actually moved "junk" from wall to wall in every room. This paid off, because we found the most of Big Mama's collection in an upstairs room. This was the bedroom that Dorothy and I first lived in when we were married in 1959. The pictures were all over the room, in the closet and on the floor. Some had even been trampled in the trash on the floor. Some had been damaged beyond recognition. I never found the two I was looking for, so I thought. In 1996, I was looking through all the pictures I brought back home when I recognized the picture of me that was taken when I was about eighteen months old. Many years ago I recall my daddy telling how he took a pack of cigarettes and placed it in my upper pocket. I kept this memory fresh over the years. Apparently, sometime along the way, I must have written the date on the back of this particular picture, because out of all the other snapshots, this was the only one marked. Someone told me that some of Herman's children, Doll's husband, might have taken some of them; when I talked to him, he said that some of the pictures might have been put in his basement and he would take a look down there, someday. Herman was about seventy when he told me this, about the same age Uncle Buddy was when he told me something similar. I doubt if he would ever look for those pictures. I planned not to pursue them any further.

The most important papers we found, in my opinion, were Uncle Buddy's court-martial papers, not all, but some. Did I say court-martial? Few people knew that Uncle Buddy had been in the Army. Very few people knew he was court-martialed or even knew what that term meant. He was court-martialed for a crime he did not commit. Arthur Jr. found these papers on Friday, and he wanted to know the story that led to that day in 1944. When I attended the Senior Noncommissioned Officer Academy in 1982, we were briefed on several subjects including having previous wrongs corrected. I even wrote down the address in Washington with Uncle Buddy in mind. I went to England right after graduation. When I returned, several obstacles stopped me from pursuing this matter any further, including Uncle Buddy's unwillingness to talk about it. If only I had known all these papers existed. Since they were among Big Mama's things, I wonder if Uncle Buddy even knew about them. But he most certainly knew about how he had been wronged.

CHAPTER FIVE

Family Devastated by the Bad News

It was September 1944 when the drama began to unfold. This particular afternoon I went to T. C.'s house. The topography of eastern Arkansas is very flat. During the period prior to the 1970s, it was heavily populated with sharecroppers' houses and dirt roads. We lived less than a quarter of a mile from Big Mama's house, shouting distance, on a straight dirt road. Often, T. C. and I spent a lot of time playing together between the two houses. As I approached the house, I could hear wailing, screaming, crying, and praying. There were Big Mama, Aunt Ethel, and a couple other ladies doing the lamenting. It seemed as if it took an hour before anyone would tell me what all the crying was about. It was probably much less. Big Mama, crying her heart out, took a short pause, leaned down to me, and said, "Your Uncle Little Buddy has killed a white man down in Georgia." I really didn't know exactly how severe that was at the time. I knew that killing any person was bad, but to be colored and kill a white person was even worse. The crying continued throughout the afternoon. Then I heard them discussing if and how they would tell Mae, my mother. Mom appeared to have been sick for some time. I learned later from reading these papers that the illness was not necessarily illness, but she was expecting a baby. All this took place just before my brother Lee was born, on September 28, 1944. She was actually in bed when they told her; the crying started all over again. I don't remember the exact day of the week, but that event that took place on that warm September afternoon in 1944 is still vivid in my mind.

A few days later or what may have been only a couple of days, I noticed Papa (my grandfather, Isaac Willie McDonald) was dressed up in a suit with his John B. Stetson hat on. Something was very important when he dressed up like this. He and Big Mama were on their way to Atlanta to see Uncle Little Buddy. They might have been present for the court-martial.

I still wonder what kind of conversation took place between them as they made that long bus ride to Atlanta. They first had to get to Hughes and then to Memphis. I seemed to recall Dad giving them some kind of instructions when they were leaving, or he might have secured a ride for them. There were not any cars in our neck of the woods back then, just mules, wagons, and lots of walking.

"Now, Ella," as Papa used to call her. "We better get going because if we miss our connection in Hughes, we might not get another bus until tomorrow."

"I know, Willie, it's just been so hard the last few days, with my boy down there in Georgia. No telling what they have already done to him."

Days, weeks, and months went by. I don't recall when they returned from Georgia. I am sure they must have told Mom and Dad what took place while they were there. On occasions I would hear my aunts talking about Uncle Little Buddy. I heard them mention that they had already hanged the other "colored" guy who was with Uncle Little Buddy when the killing took place. I even heard them say that Uncle Buddy had said that this guy was the one who actually killed the man and Uncle Buddy just happened to be with him. I concluded that there was a lot of truth to that as I read over the court-martial papers and the correspondence that we found. Even this week, June 1997, I read in the paper about President Clinton upgrading a black gentleman's dishonorable discharge to honorable. According to the paper, this man was dishonorably discharged in 1944 for stealing a small food item (I think that was the crime). If Uncle Buddy had committed the crime he was accused of, he most certainly would have been hanged as the other guy was.

CHAPTER SIX

The Court Martial

The following are excerpts of some of the papers we found. The first one is the original charge of murder:

CHARGE: Violation of the 92nd Article of War.

    Specification: In that Private Allen M. McDonald, Company A, Service Battalion, First Student Training Regiment, The Infantry School, Fort Benning, Georgia and Private Curn L. Jones, Company "A", Service Battalion, Second Student Training Regiment, The Infantry School, Fort Benning, Georgia did, at or near Columbus, Georgia, on or about 30 August 1944, with malice aforethought, willfully, deliberately, feloniously, unlawfully, and premeditation kill one Private First Class Dooley E. Parnell, Second Company, Officer Candidate Reception Unit, The Infantry School, Fort Benning, Georgia, a human being, by cutting him on the body with a sharp instrument". The charges sheet list fifteen individuals against the accused and none for. It was signed by First Lieutenant Thomas R. McLaughlin, September 5, 1944, as the accuser and investigator. This document was endorsed and referred for trial to Captain Woodrow W. Adkins, Trial Judge Advocate for General court-martial, Special Orders Number 220, September 12, 1944.

The stage was now set for the general court-martial, which took place on September 29, 1944, a month after the alleged crime. It is not known what kind of representation he had. As I mentioned above, I don't know if Grandpa and Grandma were there for the trial. The General Court-Martial Order Number 109, dated March 27, 1945, repeated the above charges. He pleaded not guilty to the charges but was found guilty and sentenced "to be hanged by the neck until dead." The sentence was approved by Major General Fred L. Walker, Commandant, U. S. Army. The following excerpt is from the court-martial orders:

> The sentence having been approved by the reviewing authority, the record of trial forwarded for the action of the President, and the record of trial having been examined by the board of Review in The Judge Advocate General's Office; and the Board of Review having submitted its opinion in writing to The Judge Advocate General, and the record of trial, the opinion of the Board of Review, and recommendation of The Judge Advocate General having been transmitted directly to the Secretary of War for the action of the President, and having been laid before the President, the following are his orders:
> "In the foregoing case of Private First Class Allen M. McDonald (37103369), Company A, Service Battalion, First Student Training Regiment, The Infantry School, Fort Benning, Georgia, the sentence is confirmed but com-

muted to dishonorable discharge, forfeiture of all pay and allowances due or to become due, and to be confinement at hard labor for life. As thus modified the sentence will be carried into execution."

FRANKLIN D. ROOSEVELT
THE WHITE HOUSE

Mar. 20, 1945

The United States Penitentiary, Atlanta, Georgia, is designated as the place of confinement.

BY ORDERS OF THE SECRETARY OF WAR

G.C. MARSHALL
Chief of Staff
OFFICIAL

CHAPTER SEVEN

The Letters

We then had a span of three years not knowing what happened between the above court-martial, March 1945, and June 1948. Based on the letters that I now have, Big Mama did not just sit idly by since she first got the news back in 1944. The following letter is the only one that seems to have started a trail. Since it uses the pronoun "his," one can assume that there were other letters prior to this one. This letter was in Big Mama's handwriting. There is no date:

> I'm asking is it possible that I may contain
> the papers of his trial or am I asking too much.

I would guess that this was part of a letter written to Congressmen Oren Harris and Ezekiel C. Gathings. Both men were in the House of Representatives from the state of Arkansas during this period. Congressman Gathings served in the Congress from 1939 to 1969. Congressman Harris served from 1941 to 1953 and then became a federal judge. Based on the date of Congressman Gathings's letter, this was one of her first letters.

Next two letters:

> Dear Mrs. McDonald: Your letter of June
> 6th has been referred to me by the Honorable
> Oren Harris as I represent the District in which

you reside. I note that you are desirous of obtaining information regarding your son, Allen, and also you request assistance in anything that can be done in his behalf. If you will send me his full name, service number and any other pertinent facts which would help identify him, I will be glad to take the matter up with the proper officials

With kind regards and best wishes, I am, Yours cordially.
/signed/ E. C. Gathings, Congressman,
First District, Arkansas
dated June 10, 1948

One may have thought that this was the end, but Grandma Luella never gave up. It is very obvious that she was a strong woman. She was born in Mississippi in 1899. I don't recall hearing her talk about her grandparents, but they had to have been slaves. I knew her mother and stepfather. Big Mama's maiden name was Curtis. She was the oldest of a half brother, Washington Ford, whom we called Uncle Son, and other half brothers and sisters whose last names were Bridges. In 1943, there was another light-skinned older gentleman who worked around McNeil's plantation house. We called him Cousin Red, but Dad would often refer to him as Red Curtis. There are no details of how this came about. It appears to me that blacks just weren't into talking about things of that nature or even family history. I wonder if we would have listened if we had been told. One thing I do know is Big Mama believed in education. She was a high school graduate; and her oldest daughter, Aunt Essie, also was a high school graduate. Her youngest daughter, Everlyn, was valedictorian of her 1947 class at Lincoln High School, Forrest City, Arkansas. Everlyn also attended Philander Smith College in Little Rock. I recall her telling us that some of the students at this college did not believe in God. Imagine that! Compare that now to 2017.

Today, it isn't saying a lot to say a black person graduated from high school, but in the latter part of the nineteenth century and early twentieth century, it was. She was a smart lady. This is evidenced by some of the letters she wrote to various dignitaries requesting help for her son who was wrongly convicted. Not only were they well written, they also prompted responses. At a recent family reunion, I commented to one of my cousins, Barbara Bridges who at one time lived with Big Mama, that she might have even written to President Roosevelt. Barbara confirmed what I suspected. We did not find any correspondence to or from the president other than the one in which he changed the sentence from death to life in prison.

> Dear Mrs. McDonald: As Mr. Gathings is in Arkansas at the present time, I am taking the liberty of acknowledging receipt of your letter regarding your son, Allen M. McDonald. This office is today contacting the Department of the Army, over Mr. Gathings' signature, requesting that a full report be submitted to us. Just as soon as it has been received, I will write you promptly. Assuring you that Mr. Gathings is delighted to be of assistance whenever possible, and with best wishes, I am, Yours sincerely,

> Judy Jones for Mr. Gathings

The above letter was dated June 23, 1948. Apparently, Mr. Gathings was still unavailable, and Judy Jones could have been acting by communicating with him by telephone because the next letter was also signed by Judy Jones for Mr. Gathings:

> Dear Mrs. McDonald: With further reference to your recent correspondence with this office concerning your son, Allen Marion McDonald, I am attaching hereto a letter which

has been received from the Department of the Army. I know that Mr. Gathings will regret to learn that Allen was not granted clemency as a result of the last review of his case; however, if you will call this matter to the attention of this office again in January 1949, we will be glad to again contact the Department in your son's behalf. Assuring you or Mr. Gathings' desire to be of assistance whenever possible, and with best wishes, I am, Cordially yours,

Judy Jones for Mr. Gathings

The letter Judy referred to from the Army was from the Special Staff of the Department of the Army, signed by a Colonel John P. Dinsmore. Colonel Dinsmore quoted a letter his office received from the adjutant general. It seems that at this point, someone began to realize that this man should not be in prison at all. But also keep in mind this is 1948 in the south. I can imagine the questions that were being raised along the route, from Congressman Gathings's office to Atlanta, as to why this congressman was trying to help a Negro family whose son had been convicted of murdering a white man. I would like to have asked Congressman Gathings the same question, because Negroes couldn't vote and, from all the evidence I have, it was his action that caused Uncle Buddy to be released from prison in 1951. Next letter:

DEPARTMENT OF THE ARMY, **SPECIAL STAFF, UNITED STATES ARMY, WASHINGTON 25, D. C.**

Dear Mr. Gathings: Permit me to refer to the interest you have expressed in General Prison Allen Marion McDonald, and the letter to you from the mother of this general prisoner, Mrs.

Luella McDonald, General Delivery, Parkin, Arkansas, which was referred by you to this Division and which is herewith returned. Mrs. McDonald solicits your assistance in her son's behalf. As the result of an inquiry initiated by this Division, a report has been received from The Adjutant General which is quoted for your information, as follows:

Quote, Reference is made to your memorandum of 29 June 1948 enclosing a copy of a letter to Honorable E. C. Gathings from Mrs. Luella McDonald, General Delivery, Parkin, Arkansas, regarding her son, General Prison Allen M. McDonald, Army serial number 37103369. The records show that Private First Class Allen M. McDonald was tried by general court martial and found guilty, unquote.

The quote went on to repeat all the charges that the general court-martial orders listed. I will skip this part and go on:

Quote, As the result of favorable clemency action on this general prisoner's behalf, his sentence to confinement was reduced to twenty-five years. His subsequent annual review resulted in the further reduction to twenty years. The Warden, United States Penitentiary, Atlanta, Georgia, had been informed of these decisions by blue seal communications dated 4 March 1946 and 30 January 1947. As the result of the last review of his case, clemency was disapproved on 28 January 1948. His return to military duty is not favorably considered. In accordance with

Army regulations, his next annual review is scheduled to be held in January 1949. Unquote.

Sincerely yours,

JOHN P. DINSMORE, Colonel, CSG,
Special Assistant to the Chief Legislative and
Liaison Division 49

For whatever reason, this same letter was also sent to Congressman Oren Harris, who had earlier referred Big Mama's first letter to Congressman Gathings. To gain votes from blacks was not at issue here, but something was. Big Mama was still not pleased with the action of Congressman Gathings or the Army. Apparently, she had also communicated with the Army that prompted this reply from General Witsell:

> War Department, 6 January 1949, Dear Mrs. McDonald: I am sorry that my reply to your letter concerning the general prisoner named below has been unavoidably delayed: Allen M. McDonald, Army Serial Number 37103369. Case is being reviewed for clemency. The matter is receiving attention, and as soon as I have the necessary information, I will reply to your request. Sincerely yours, Edward F. Witsell.

The letters continues:

> Congress of the United States, December 30, 1948, Dear Mrs. McDonald: This is to acknowledge receipt of your letter of December 24 with reference to your son, Allen Marion McDonald. I am at this time writing the Adjutant General of the Army, General Edward F. Witsell,

Urging that your son be given every possible consideration when his case is reviewed in January of 1949. I am enclosing herewith a copy of my letter to him. As soon as I hear from him, I will advise you at once. With assurance that it is a pleasure for me to be of service to you in connection with this matter and with best wishes, I am Yours sincerely, E. C. Gathings.

The following is the letter Congressman Gathings wrote to General Witsell:

December 30, 1948, Dear General Witsell: I am writing in the interest of General Prison, Allen Marion McDonald, who is serving a sentence in the Federal penitentiary at Atlanta, Georgia of twenty five years. A review of his case was made on the 28th of January, 1948 in which it was recommended that his return to military duty not be favorably considered. I have a letter dated August 17, 1948 from Colonel John P. Dinsmore stating that the next annual review of Mr. McDonald's case would be in January of 1949. In view of the fact that this prisoner has been confined for many years, I trust that you will see fit to further reduce his sentence. Thanking you and with kind regards, I am Yours sincerely, E. C. Gathings.

Unfortunately, and I suppose to the disappointment of Big Mama, this reply was received concerning the above two letters:

Department of the Army, 4 February 1949, Honorable E. C. Gathings, House of Representatives, "Dear Mr. Gathings: I again refer to your letter concerning General Prisoner Allen M. McDonald, Army serial number 37103369. McDonald's sentence was reduced to twenty years as the result of his annual review in January 1947. When his case was considered in January 1948, both clemency and his return to a military duty status were not favorably considered. At the review just completed it was found that justice would best be served by not granting the extension of clemency. His case is schedule for its next annual review in January 1950. With best wishes, Sincerely Yours, EDWARD F. WITSELL, Major General, The Adjutant General.

One of the most puzzling letters was the next one, written in long hand:

May 5/1951. "Mrs. McDonald,
     You will probably be surprise & wonder who wrote to you.
     I am doing this for your son Allen in Atlanta & I wish it to be kept in the strictest confidence.
     When you write to him please don't mention the contents of this letter. Everything is censored & investigated & maybe cause him & I trouble. Just write & tell him that an old army friend of his they called (Dago) from Pgh. Wrote to you and inquired about him.
     That's the arrangement we made a long time ago before I left Atlanta. He is getting along fine hope to go up for parole next year. He is a good boy & has made a good-record in Atlanta & should make parole. But in the event he don't you can write to Walter Winchell in NY and ask him for the name of that ex judge who can get

a man out legally after serving one third of his time. He would like to see you but it makes him feels bad when you leave that he don't wish to see you soon.

I intended to come see you in person but circumstances will not allow it at the present.

If anyone comes to you saying that they can get Allen out don't believe it.

All these societies and organizations are just a racket. Allen told me what all you done to get him out. Don't give no one money until you see your son knocking on your front door.

I am a white boy & taking a chance writing to you but I promised Little Bro. That I would.

I don't know for sure whether that man can help you or not but I believe if you state your case properly he may be able to.

I don't believe your son belongs in prison. He didn't do anything to go there in the first place.

I make doubly sure I had someone else write this and I am not sending you my name. Not that I don't trust you. If you all are alike your son you are very nice.

Don't forget you may get him in trouble if you report this.

The letter was unsigned.

Who was Dago? Where was he from? The letters Pgh don't help a lot. He suggested that she contact Walter Winchell and ask him to contact the ex-judge. I Goggled Walter Winchell. Based on what was written about him, he probably could have stirred some positive action. These are names of people who were probably up in age in 1950. It is doubtful if any are still alive. Keep in mind that the next review was to be "January 1950." Apparently parole was denied. The above letter could have sparked a new twist for Grandma to take, contacting that ex-judge in New York, or further action by Congressman Gathings.

Aunt Ethel, Uncle Buddy's next to the youngest sister, was about age fourteen when all this first started back in 1944 and culminated in 1951. She would not shed any light on the subject when I talked to her in the mid-1990s, although her mind was still sharp as ever. On September 6, 2000, my sister, Melverdia, called to inform me Aunt Ethel had passed. She was the last of that generation. She was seventy years old.

It was the summer of 1951, perhaps a Sunday. We were still living in "33," but in a different house, closer to the highway. A car pulled up in the yard. Before it came to a complete stop, Aunt Everlyn whom we called "Doll" jumped out of the car and asked us children "Who is this man?" pointing to Uncle Little Buddy who was exiting the car about this time. I don't recall the answer that was given or who gave it. We all rejoiced that Uncle Little Buddy was out of prison. At age thirty-one when he was released, his new life had begun.

I wish I could have thanked Congressman Gathings personally. With the exception of the personal letter from "Dago," no other correspondence mentioned that Uncle Allen had been wrongfully convicted. I supposed that political correctness was even at play in 1944. Wrongfully convicted was not even mentioned in any of the congressman's letters. You just don't commit first-degree murder and get paroled in seven years.

CHAPTER EIGHT

His New Life

As I look back to 1944, I was only six years old. In 1951 when Uncle Buddy was released, I was thirteen. That's a long time in the life of a youngster. I suppose it was a long time for Uncle Buddy as well. Seven years had been taken from him for something he didn't do. But I never heard him complain about it. On the other hand, he never talked about it either. He did love to talk about the Army, with pride and smiles. I recall talking to him shortly before I joined the Air Force. We were up late that night. I had a lot of questions about military life. Nobody knew I was planning on enlisting, not even my wife. Admittedly, that was not so smart.

He even told me about how Uncle James, his brother, was also in the Army shortly after he had been drafted. He told of how James would dress as an officer. He said that James even came to visit him once dressed as an officer. This was before he got into trouble. I even recall Uncle James coming home on furlough and staying a long time. I found out later that he was absent without leave (AWOL). I heard Dad mention something about it sometime later how James had relayed the story to him that when they finally caught him he went to jail and how he had awakened and found himself on a ship heading overseas.

A lot of young Negroes were drafted during World War II. I used to listen to conversations up at the company store of who had received their notice to report to the military draft board for evaluation. Those who qualified locally were transferred to induction centers and I suppose to military training. I recall when Dad received his notice. Mom starched his only decent-looking pair of green trousers. Off he went, not knowing if they would keep him or not. I think this was in 1945. There were at least six of us children at the time, the oldest being twelve. I don't remember if it was before or after our sister, Ruby, had died. Needless to say, they sent him back home, probably based on that fact along.

One condition of Uncle Buddy's parole was that he had to stay in Arkansas. For how long I don't know. He lived near Parkin, close to his parents, for a while. His wife, Ethel, whom he had married prior to the trouble, remarried while he was in prison. I don't know if there was a divorce or not. I don't think the law was enforced real close when it came to Negroes in the south in situation as marriages and divorces.

He soon married a little dark woman who could be described like the woman in Tony Joe White's song "Polk Salad Annie," "a mean, razor totting woman." They abused each other pretty bad. Needless to say, they weren't together very long. Things did not end for him there. Somehow, he and his first wife got back together. I don't know who found whom. I think she and her husband were living in Memphis at the time Uncle Little Buddy was released from prison. I don't know what happened to her other husband or to Uncle Little Buddy's second wife. It was rumored that she had deserted him when he received the life sentence. In any event they got back together sometime during the mid-1950s and moved to Davenport, Iowa. It might have been after he moved to Davenport that they got back together.

He got a job with the Buick dealer in Davenport shortly after he arrived and worked there until he retired shortly before his death. I mentioned earlier that he was a hard worker. He also had a lot of pride in what he did, and he didn't mind boasting about it. I remember the first time I went to Davenport; he took me to his job. He showed off the wash stall where he would first wash a car and then the area where he would wax and detail it. If it was a new car and needed undercoating, he showed me where this took place also.

He appeared to have enjoyed everything he did. He didn't make a lot of money, but he spent wisely. He got good deals on used Buicks. When I first moved to Davenport in 1958, he had a beautiful green 1951 Buick Special. It was that same year that he called me about a 1951 Buick Super, gray and white, that just had been traded in. He came and picked me up and took me down to the dealership, and I bought my first car ever for $425.00.

One vice that I knew he had early on there in Davenport was women. I heard someone say that Ethel knew it existed but, because of what she did while he was in prison, looked the other way.

He loved all his family, not just brothers and sisters, but nieces, nephews, aunts, uncles, and in-laws. I can honestly say that I never detected any favoritism from him among the many relatives that knew him. He was a well-loved individual. When I first came to Davenport during the summer of 1958, he and Ethel owned the house at 1116 West 5th Street, the same house that he was living in when he died. I think all the Phillips's children who eventually moved to Davenport spent some time in one of those little rooms upstairs in this house and nearly rent free. He was the mainstay behind Big Mama and Papa leaving Arkansas and moving to Davenport. He even purchased a house for them to live in on Grand Avenue. It wasn't much, but it was shelter and he and his parents loved it. He seemed so happy with everything and/or every feat he set out and accomplished.

I had a conservation with my cousin, Barbara Bridges, about the letters Grandma Luella had written to various dignitaries request-ing assistance. Barbara, who lived with Grandma Luella for a period, stated that "she also wrote letters to President Roosevelt and per-haps to President Truman". However, I believe that Congressman Gathings was the impetus behind having Uncle Little Buddy released from prison. The following is a brief biography of Ezekiel Candler Gathings, copied from the Biographical Directory of the United States Congress: "He was born in Prairie, Monroe County, Mississippi, November 10, 1903; attended the public schools and the University of Alabama at Tuscaloosa; was graduated from the law department of the University of Arkansas at Fayetteville in 1929; was admitted to the bar the same year and commenced practice in Helena, Arkansas; moved to West Memphis, Arkansas, in 1932 and continued the practice of law; served in the State senate 1935-1939; elected as a Democrat to the Seventy-sixth and to the fourteen succeeding Congresses (January 3, 1939-January 3, 1969); was not a candidate for reelection in 1968 to the Ninety-first Congress; resumed the practice of law; served as a member of West Memphis, Ark., Port Authority; resided in West Memphis, Arkansas., where he died May 2, 1979; interment in Crittenden Memorial Park, Marion, Arkansas" (Reference, www.bioguide.congress.gov).

ABOUT THE AUTHOR

Arthur Phillips is a retired Air Force senior master sergeant. He grew up in rural eastern Arkansas where cotton was the primary crop. However, soy beans, wheat, and oats were also grown. He attended Lincoln High School in Forrest City, Arkansas, where he lettered in football and baseball. He received a football scholarship from Philander Smith College, Little Rock, Arkansas, but turned it down and moved to Davenport, Iowa. He later sent for his high school sweetheart, and they were married in 1959. Shortly thereafter, he enlisted in the Air Force. His military duties had taken him to several countries and travels throughout the United States. He currently lives with his wife in Nebraska. They have four children. Two of his favorite phrases are "Grow where you are planted" and "Be responsible for your own actions." One of Arthur's favorite scriptures is Ecclesiastes 12:13.

Printed in the USA
CPSIA information can be obtained
at www.ICGtesting.com
CBHW081930091223
2508CB00006B/36

9 781642 585124